MIRRAN THOUGHT

MIRRAN THOUGHT
Spitzwiesenstr. 50
90765 Fürth
Germany

www.dwmirran.de
www.empty.de
empty@empty.de

READ TWENTYFIVE
(MT-632)

Production and publishing: BOD - Books on Demand, Norderstedt
ISBN: 978-3-7534-2787-4

First printing 2021

MIRRAN THOUGHT is the publishing arm of Mirran Threat, a company devoted to releasing the music and writings of the various members of Doc Wör Mirran. Mirran Thought and Mirran Threat are both divisions of MT Undertainment.

4

In God We Trusted

Joseph B. Raimond

Written in Fürth in 2016.

As always, in loving memory of Frank
Abendroth and Tom Murphy.

For Conny, my perfect angel

Dedicated to Meredith Hunter

Cover art by Joseph B. Raimond
"In God We Trusted" watercolor and
ink on paper, 2016 Fürth

This is DWM release Nr. 182

In God We Trusted

In God we trusted
When we were little, naïve
Stupid
Forced to stand at attention
Forced to put our hand on our heart
And forced to pledge our allegiance

In god we trusted
Until we grew up
And looked at the world
And saw the reality
And saw the cruelty
Of what our nation was capable of

What does this mean, if
We really were
Created in god's own image?

No, I'm turning my back
On your twisted interpretations
Your red, white and blue arrogance
And your endless demands
For blind patriotism

No, I'm turning my back
On your legions of racists
Your armies of fascists

Your proud boy militias
And your perverse definition
Of freedom

And you know what?
God,
Is on my side!

The Human Spectrum

A poet's few words, wisdom entwined
Tears will flow as the music inspires
And touches our humble soul
The painting leaps forth,
The power of color and form
Rips at our very being, demands
Our humanity rises to
Stellar heights
To briefly touch heaven

A little girl's decapitated head
Presented on a pole as a token
Mass graves of rotting bodies
Names no longer with meaning
From hand-guns to nuclear bombs
Man's instruments of hatred
Express the twisted interpretations
Of his holy books
While our humanity sinks
To the depths of hell itself

The American Fool

Very little
In this world of fools
Seems quite so foolish
As the old man sitting
Writing poetry

I am fully aware of this

And as you sit
And instead watch your television
Consuming your fast-food culture
Feeding your hunger for
Scripted reality show tears
And sitcom pre-recorded laugh tracks for
Jokes that are never funny

I sit here and write
And compile
My little books
That you will never read

I Will Never Be A Marlboro Man

while waiting for the bus, the gaudy billboard asks me in its typical offensively vile marketing fashion "where will you go from here?" as if the marketing slime who thought up this piece of fine literature would really ever care, but to answer his or her slimy marketing style question the answer is "to work", and certainly not into some store somewhere to buy whatever deathly, cancer inducing, habit forming "product" you are trying to sell!

Breasts And Ass Blood

the cleavage monster
attacks the sexists of the world
without mercy
the men and women scream from their
ugly genitals, now mutilated

ass blood oozes guilt
it takes two to tango
in ugly rectum square dancing halls
behind closed, Christian doors
hushed, but with a wink
of the republican eye

this is, after all,
an election year

meanwhile, another bible belt bastard
is busy raping his grandson
as the television evangelist
begging for cash, phony preaching
on channel six six six

a good Christian, he won't forget
to send him a twenty tomorrow

Equality

Driving around in your hundred thousand
Dollar wheels
That nagging melancholy
Is just as good
At getting you to feel like shit
As it is with me
Driving in my little Volks

That dark grey cloud of gloom
Is just as good at raining on your
Multimillion dollar roof
As it is at raining on my
Semi-detached roof

Don't think you are anything better
Both the doom and the gloom
And I
We all know that darkness
All too well

And you can try to hide behind your
Stuff!
But the pleading sadness in your eyes
Shines louder than your arrogance
It gives you away
As another lonely soul

Leaping towards death
As fast and painfully
As the rest of us

For Drumpf

Selma was a good fuck
So was Marion
(Gabi wasn't though!)

So, why am I allowed to say this
And you aren't?

Because I am not trying to become
President
I wouldn't take the job anyway
No matter what the pay

Also,
I am not a sexist, racist, ugly pig
Like you

I only wrote this poem this way
Because it is the only kind of language
You would ever understand

Is dumbed-down art, that is
Art brought down to your level
Still art?

Let Me Go

Just let me go
I never was fire
And flame
For you anyway
So just let me go

Always too unrealistic
Too uncompromising
Too unpatriotic
So just let me go

Never blind enough
I saw and sought
Your weaknesses and your
Injustices
I was always ready
To call you out
To throw your phony
Democracy back in your face
So please, just let me go

Too idealistic
I could never accept
Your blind patriotism
Waving your red white and blue in my face
Without question

So please, just let me go
It is better for both of us

The American Train

Dear world
I am so, so sorry
For what I have done
And although I may regret
My vicious actions,
You may pity me
But don't ever forgive me

I know,
You thought you knew me
But you don't know shit
As I pretended
To offer you my hand
I was in reality
Just trying to steal your wallet
But like the cheap Walmart
Plastic Halloween costume
If you looked hard enough
You could have seen
My true identity

For this is only the beginning
As I have given all the
Racists, bigots, sexists
A free ticket to the land of hate

And a new president
Along for the ride
Who is more than qualified
To represent them
Has been chosen

And having now arrived
The racists, bigots and sexists
Pat each other on the back
For a campaign well won
While the rest of the world
Stares in stunned silence

Modern Fascism

I give her the middle finger
But unfortunately,
The boobed and pretty blonde on
This insulting television commercial
Will never see
My rude gesture

I yell at the idiot newscaster
Call him insulting names
But unfortunately,
The probably well hung yet handsome
Bringer of bad news
Will never hear
What he deserves

Television
A fascist invention to keep the masses
Suppressed, where their voices of anger
Will never be heard
Outside their modest four walls

Angel Stew

Just having arrived in town
One could smell
The sour, deathly air

Gazing across the barren
Cultural wasteland
Like a deadly cancer
Upon a dying land
With its row upon row
Of identical, depressed dwellings
Augmented here and there
With a fast-food restaurant,
Gas station or shopping center
The dirty homeless
Pepper this stew of gloom and
Hopelessness

Still hungry?

November 9th, 2016

Here we go again
And I am so damn tired
Of always despising
Our commander in chief

Maybe,
There really is something
Wrong with me
Am I really so
Abnormal
Just because
I expect this nation
To do the right thing?
To see through
And fight against
Sexism, racism and bigotry
Fascism

Does democracy really mean
To let a bunch of racist
Gun-toting
Lynyrd Skynyrd listening
Pickup truck driving
Uneducated, unemployed
Backwater fucks
To vote?

If this
Is what democracy means
Well,
Then you can keep it
I want no part of it

American Mourn

Like a funeral
We are in a state of sadness
Anger, not understanding
Scorn, at your patronizing word

"The dawn of a new era"
Or
"The death of false pity"

No no no no no
Shut the fuck up

In a rage of barred teeth
I ball my fists and hereby
Declare my eternal opposition
I will fight on, and on, and on

Don't Need Rope

For every Islamic terrorist
Out there chopping off the heads
Of little Christian children
Perverting the name of his god
There is a suit and tie among us
Selling him weapons
To line his silken, blood-soaked pockets

For every gang member
Gunned down for showing his colors
There is a suit and tie among us
Protecting your rights
To produce, purchase and use guns

For every unarmed black man
Gunned down by a racist white cop
There is a suit and tie among us
Who will represent the legal rights
Of all white racist cops
To make sure they are not held
Accountable for their crimes

If you ever become gravely ill
With lung cancer
Die with the knowledge
That there is a suit and tie

Among you
Who wrote sweet and jolly little
Advertising slogans
Trying to sell you his brand of death
Just so he can afford a new car
And a cappuccino every afternoon

For every majestic elephant
Poached for his tusks
There is a suit and tie among us
Organizing the logistics
For the illegal ivory trade
So some stupid, overweight Japanese
Suit and tie
Can think he fucks his ugly fat wife better

For every one of our children
Born deformed
Missing fingers, without a healthy heart
Missing intellect
There is a suit and tie among us
Trying to hide the fact
That his company developed and sold you drugs
That caused your suffering
Just to line his pockets with the cash
He will need to pay for his coke habit

It is time we held
All the suit and ties of this world
Accountable
For their immoral actions
Don't bother fetching the rope
Their ties are already
Wrapped around their worthless necks
Ready to do the job

To The Dogs

While Republicans and Democrats
So similar anyway
Continue in their decades long
Childish political deadlock
The rest of their country
Goes to the dogs

The land of hope and glory?
What is so glorious
About standing in the soup line?
What is so glorious
About not being able to afford
Simple health care?
What is so glorious
About getting gunned down
On a grey, depressed city street?

Hope?
You're kidding, aren't you?
What did hope bring my friend Tom
Who, homeless
Killed himself in the parking lot
Of the hospital
After they refused to treat him
Turning one of the kindest
People you could ever have met

Into just another sad
American statistic

What does hope really mean
When the most you can ever hope for
Is the occasional free meal
And a warm, dry night
Spent sleeping in a dirty alley?

What does hope really mean
When the best you can hope for
Is being able to call yourself lucky
Because you work two jobs
Sixty hours a week
And only so you might
Make ends meet?

While the dumb, uneducated white
Rednecks
Fight for their God-given right
To possess as many guns as an army
Their country goes to the dogs

While the dumb, white
Television evangelist
Rakes in millions

Preaching his bastard
Perverse interpretations
Of a supposed holy book
To the dumb and depraved
Gullible
His country goes to the dogs

While the fat and divorced
Housewife devours
Her supersizes
Squalor in front of the daily
Reality show
Her country goes to the dogs

The land of hope and glory
Has turned into the land
Of hopelessness
Hunger and want

And the rest of the world
Has moved on

-ism

An -ism is always defined
By rules, regulations
That you are expected
To always follow

Patriotism vs. anarchism
Capitalism vs. communism
Liberalism vs. conservativism
Realism vs. abstract expressionism
Atheism vs. Christian fundamentalism

My –ism vs. your –ism
My –ism = good
Your –ism = bad

We seem to have
Some sort of inborn
Urge
To push all our ideas
Ideals and philosophies
Even our art
Into predefined –isms,
To catalog and categorize
To label, price
And put on sale

No thanks!

I want no part of any
Of your -isms
Stop trying to convince me
To be part of your exclusive club
As to adopt your –ism
I have to give up
A part of myself

The City

Old enough to crave the
Female body
But young enough
To be without commitments
I moved to
The City
(Following a beautiful girl
Of course!)

It took me a few days to get there
Travelling the American Midwest
Land of corn, country music
Rednecks and space
So much space
Enough space to do anything
You would ever want to do

And, finally arriving
I learned to love that city
And with a few other
Of my displaced friends
We sort of grew up there

Wandering Broadway
Too broke usually to pay the door
We'd wander up and down

Always on the move
To keep the police
And their charge of loitering
At bay

In the alleys
We'd see the rich little boys
In their daddy's cars
Sucking the titties of
The twenty dollar whores

The air was sweet
With the scent of liberal
Views of cannabis
And tolerance
Of who you wanted to love

The dark streets of North Beach
Too narrow for the American cars
Reminding me of Europe
With its little bookshops
Lined with books of poetry
From beat authors you never heard of
And a corner record store
Selling the new single
From a local band you saw last week

During the day,
I'd wander the hilly, colorful streets
Up and down, legs sore
Each ornate Victorian house
More beautiful than the last

At night
I hung around the cool bars
Hoping not to get carded
Paying my punk rock dues
Learning my lessons in life
Taught the morals that today
Define who I am

Everywhere water and the
Salty smell of the ocean
Pure blue, California skies
Warm air and my strong
Young body,
I miss my old, privileged life
In The City

An American Recipe

At your loud rally
Holding up your sign
Proudly advertising
Your dumb sloganeering
For the whole world to see
Stupidity, American-style

As you look into the camera
The whites of your eyes
Showing off
How proud you have become
As you chant your racism
American-style
For the whole world to hear

Like a horny street dog
Humping a little girl's leg
At the neighborhood playground
The world laughs,
Points
But still watches in fascination
Brainless exhibitionism
At the political perversion
You like to call democracy,
American-style

Oceans away
I see you on the television
Cringe at what tomorrow will bring
When the world again
Asks me to explain
Fast-food politics,
American style

9/11

sick firefighters setting sail for Cuba / the dust lady died a lonesome dust-free death / where were you when you heard the news? / please exit through the backdoor and watch out for falling bodies / it took them years to clear the rubble / he missed the ferry and was the only one in his company who survived / everyone knows someone who knew someone who died in the attack / it doesn't matter who we attack, as long as we get revenge! / only the Saudis were allowed to fly that day / did you see the look on Bush's face? / not all Muslims are terrorists, but all terrorists are Muslims / the US government did it to raise public support for a new US war in Iraq / I visited Ground Zero last year / they let us go home from work early that day /that kind of thing never happens in America! / Let's Rock! / did you hear? the Pentagon is burning!

Cultural Refugee

I once dodged
The city's many homeless
As they filled the hungry streets
Which are lined with
The mansions of the very rich
Who are always so very good
At looking away,
Pretending they don't see

I ducked and hid
As the local gangs
Began shooting at each other
With white murder
In their depraved eyes
And a photo-copy of their constitutional right
To carry guns tucked under
Their gang colors

As a painter
I could never understand
The American pallet
Where I was only allowed to paint
In red, white and blue

As a poet
I could never understand

My supposed freedom of speech
To write what I wanted
Just as long as
I didn't criticize
Their supposed "land of the free"

When I would be lucky
To escape
With only a "love it or leave it"
And a push to the commies and socials
Of a perverted Europe

So,
I left
Decades ago
Both in heart and soul
A land I never understood
A land that also
Never tried to understand me

So proud of their melting pot
There was no place
Left for me

#1

We the people,
Nod our patriotic heads
As we sit at the pews of church
Rows and rows of god fearing
Flag waving republican patriot lemmings
Listening to the sermons of the pastors
Through our brown paper bags
That we can't think
Our way out of

And only because
Mr. Pastor is from this church
Well, it must be moral
With god's own stamp of approval
To fear and loathe my fellow man
If only because he looks different
Thinks different
Or
God forbid
Doesn't believe in a god,
Or my god

Then we go home
Morally cleansed
With a clean slate
Ready to go back to our immoral ways

To hell with the immigrants
The poor, the lonely, the sick
Why should my tax dollars
Pay for a bunch of lazy
Deadbeats and free-loaders

After I fuck you
In a motel,
Want to drive with me
To church on Sunday?

Political Poem For Brian Ladd

How could you?
Join the masses
Of brainless stupid hate mongers
As they swim
To their moral deaths
In their swamp of stinking
Dying bigots
Pulling each other down
And drowning
In the ugly muck
Of uneducated bigotry

You've been so busy
Turning a blind eye
You must be senselessly
Dizzy by now
Spinning round and round
Your pale,
White male
Palms must be sore and red
From all the redneck
High-fiving
You've been so busy doing lately
With all your buddy bros!

If you have to have a dumb
Ugly and heartless
-ism
To define what you have become
Well, go ahead and choose
There are enough of them flying around
In the wake of your disaster
To choose from

It would have been so easy
For me,
To just rant and rave
Insult you,
Like I have grown tired
Of doing with so many others
In the wake of your disaster

When the word liberal
Is spat like
Any other four letter word
When pity and empathy
Are considered emotions
Of the weak
And hate is considered cool

But the fact is,
I admired you once
I collected your art,
Honestly listened to what you
As an artist had to say
So instead of hate, and anger,
Emotions I'll let you go ahead and keep,
I just feel honest
Disappointment .

And by the way,
I threw out all your albums

American Idol

Jump out, jump in
Jump into the mouth
Of the hungry monster

Economic livestock that you are
Let yourself be
Led to the intellectual slaughter
Sold for stupid
At pennies per pound
And while you are being devoured
Supersized that you are
By the never satiated
Sold on that new car
Don't forget to buy that new
Limited edition dash
With mint aroma
Only while supplies last!
Pick up a burger or two
At the drive thru
On your way home
Then a six-pack and a box of smokes
While you consume
In your naïve innocence
Another American idol
The real monster
Is consuming you

How Dared You?

How dared you
Judge me so
With your phony morals
And blind, unquestioning patriotism
Claiming I was a pussy whipped European
Did you honestly think
I should have turned out like you?

Blind to your nation's ignorance
Blind to humanity's hunger
Blind to your neighbor's squalor
Blind to your friend's disease
Blind to your family's love

Blind to your own holy book

When you were hardly ever there
Between your holy prayers
And out fucking your secretary
And when you were there
You were never there
For me

Red, White and Blue

Pushing old age, but
Opening my eyes
Like a newborn baby
I resolve never to overestimate you again
Never to employ false hope
The disease was set long ago
Terminal in your stupidity
And there is no hope
For your diseased, immoral soul
And I am no doctor either
With a miracle cure
And I am no nurse
Ready to nurse you in your
Long road towards
Your inevitable death
Of squalor and want
Wiping your ass as you shit
Your stupid words of idiocy
While you assume
You are too good, too god chosen
To clean up your own shit-smeared mess
So you continue to defecate your immorality
All the while waving proud
Your shit stained
Red, white and blue

Inferiorists

Have you ever noticed
That white supremacists
Are usually fat,
Butt-ugly,
Gun toting (penis prothesis)
Uneducated, redneck morons?
In short,
They are the least supreme examples
Their race can offer

Dude,
Look in a mirror
Do you actually like
What you see?

Burn

Go ahead,
Burn this book,
The fire is roaring again
And I know how much you missed it

Go ahead,
Douse the paper in gasoline
Savor the smell
Of the devil's work
This depraved, socialist
Liberal propaganda
Masquerading as art
About to be destroyed

Now strike the match
And light up the midnight sky
As it reflects in your hollow eyes
And the white hoods
Of your racist uniforms

I would be in
Good company

Old Joe

old joe would be proud of you
witch hunting in the
great american tradition
although killing commies
for mommies has gone the way
of the journey by train
america always needs
its bad guys, television
and church sermons to keep
its people dumb and complacent
today it isn't the commies we fear
but the terrorists
so let's begin the hunt!
fetch the rope
consume a few alternate facts
close our eyes
so we are blind to truth
put our hands over our ears
and not listen to the voice
of empathy or reason
cover our mouths
so we won't come up
with the crazy idea
of utilizing our theoretical
freedom of speech
old joe would be proud of you

Fascism, American Style

(sing along to the tune of "Love, American Style!")

Fascism, fascism, fascism

Fascism, American Style,
Shaming the Red, White and Blue.
Fascism, American Style,
That's not me, is it you?

And on a blood splattered night my love,
(My conscience came to me).
I will resist their fake news
See through their alternate facts
As I defend my right to overcome.

Fascism, American Style,
That's not me, is it you?

Make America Again

Make America dumb again
Make America lame again
Make America Republican again
Make America homophobic again
Make America sexist again
Make America racist again
Make America bigoted again
Make America stupid again
Make America laughable again
Make America dirty again
Make America sad again
Make America corrupt again
Make America homeless again
Make America sick again
Make America hungry again
Make America poor again
Make America helpless again
Make America weak again

You have accomplished so much,
In fact, almost everything
Except to make America great again

The Fuckshits

Why?
Why bother?
Why bother trying anymore?
Just let the fuckshits
Do whatever they want
And let's just end this whole shebang
It's almost not worth the trouble
Anymore

Like the spoiled
Depressed 27 year-old rock star
Hell-bent on sending himself
To hell
With a bullet through his
Lame-brained
Grey matter

Just let the republican fuckshits
Do whatever they want
Go ahead, build your pipeline
Through holy land
Go ahead, buy more tanks
More bombers, more guns
Go ahead, more immoral stuff
Put more and more money
In each other's pockets

Go ahead, protect the profits
Of all your suits and ties
Go ahead, reduce our rights
Pull more wool
Over our crying eyes

Or, go ahead,
Just push the big red button
Blow us all to smithereens
And let's be done with it quick
And do this planet
One final, big favour

Cheeto

Go ahead
Thump
The orange tRumple bump
And put it out
Of our misery

The Cheeto is stale
Mushy and mold
Take it out of our plastic bag
and
Throw it back into the swamp
Where it came from
And put it out
Of our misery

A Song For America

(sing along to the tune of "My Country 'Tis of Thee")

My country, 'tis of thee
Sweet land of misery
To thee I not cling
The land where my father died
Wallowed in his nationalistic pride
This sickness spreads now countrywide
No freedom rings

My naïve country, thee
Land of the pseudo free
Thy ideals I mourn
I loathe thy guns of death
The labs for crystal meth
Where happiness has no breath
In Christianity reborn

As racists rape the breeze,
Their noose hangs from the trees
No black man's freedom song;
Let mortal ugly tongues wag;
From the Walmart housewife hags
Their husband's fat fingers gag
Their stench prolong.

Our father's God left thee,
The authors of liberty,

Turn in their graves
Long will your land be blight,
In moral darkness there is no light,
I turn my back to you tonight
Forever walk away